DINOSAUR PROFILES

GIGANOTOSAURUS

Titles in the Dinosaur Profiles series include:

DINOSAUR PROFILES

GIGANOTOSAURUS

Text by Fabio Marco Dalla Vecchia
Illustrations by Leonello Calvetti and Luca Massini

BLACKBIRCH PRESS

An imprint of Thomson Gale, a part of The Thomson Corporation

THOMSON
★
GALE

Detroit • New York • San Francisco • New Haven, Conn. • Waterville, Maine • London

THOMSON

GALE

For more information, contact
The Gale Group, Inc.
27500 Drake Rd.
Farmington Hills, MI 48331-3535
Or you can visit our Internet site at http://www.gale.com

Computer illustrations 3D and 2D: Leonello Calvetti and Luca Massini

Photographs: page 21, Fabio Marco Dalla Vecchia

LIBRARY OF CONGRESS CATALOGING-IN-PUBLICATION DATA

Dalla Vecchia, Fabio Marco.
Giganotosaurus / text by Fabio Marco Dalla Vecchia ; illustrations by Leonello Calvetti and Luca Massini.
    p. cm.—(Dinosaur profiles)
Includes bibliographical references and index.
ISBN-13: 978-1-4103-0735-4 (hardcover)
ISBN-10: 1-4103-0735-2 (hardcover)
1. Giganotosaurus—Juvenile literature. I. Calvetti, Leonello, ill. II. Massini, Luca, ill. III. Title.

QE862.S3D395 2007
567.912—dc22

2006102172

Printed in the United States of America
10 9 8 7 6 5 4 3 2 1

CONTENTS

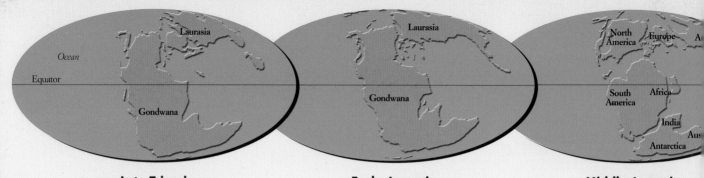

Late Triassic
228–206 million years ago

Early Jurassic
206–176 million years ago

Middle Jurassic
176–161 million years

A Changing World

Earth's long history began 4.6 billion years ago. Dinosaurs are some of the most fascinating animals from the planet's long past.

The word *dinosaur* comes from the word *dinosauria*. This word was invented by the English scientist Richard Owen in 1842. It comes from two Greek words, *deinos* and *sauros*. Together, these words mean "terrifying lizard."

The dinosaur era, also called the Mesozoic era, lasted from 228 million years ago to 65 million years ago. It is divided into three periods. The first, the Triassic period, lasted 42 million years. The second, the Jurassic period, lasted 61 million years. The third, the Cretaceous period, lasted 79 million years. Dinosaurs ruled the world for a huge time span of 160 million years.

Like dinosaurs, mammals appeared at the end of the Triassic period. During the time of dinosaurs, mammals were small animals the size of a mouse. Only after dinosaurs became extinct did mammals develop into the many forms that exist today. Humans never met Mesozoic dinosaurs. The dinosaurs were gone nearly 65 million years before humans appeared on Earth.

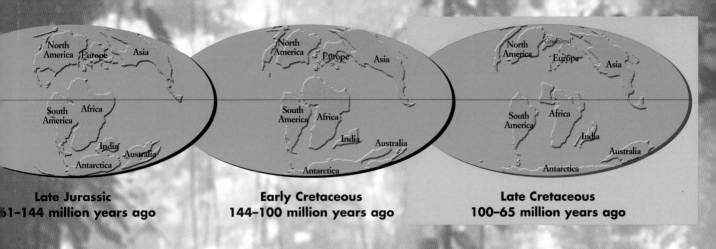

Late Jurassic
61–144 million years ago

Early Cretaceous
144–100 million years ago

Late Cretaceous
100–65 million years ago

Dinosaurs changed in time. Stegosaurus and Brachiosaurus no longer existed when Tyrannosaurus and Triceratops appeared 75 million years later.

The dinosaur world was different from today's world. The climate was warmer, with few extremes. The position of the continents was different. Plants were constantly changing, and grass did not even exist.

A Huge Predator

Giganotosaurus was an enormous meat-eating dinosaur that lived in what is now the South American country of Argentina. The name *Giganotosaurus* comes from Greek and means "giant southern lizard."

This dinosaur was even bigger than Tyrannosaurus rex. An adult Giganotosaurus weighed as much as 8 tons (7.3 metric tons). It was 39 to 45 feet (12 to 13.7m) long and 12 feet (3.7m) tall. It was bipedal, meaning it walked on its two hind legs.

Giganotosaurus lived in the middle of the Cretaceous period, 100 to 95 million years ago. This dinosaur was related to Carcharodontosaurus, which lived in northern Africa. It was also related to Achrochantosaurus, which lived in what are now Oklahoma and Texas. Because Giganotosaurus was related to these other dinosaurs, some scientists believe that a land bridge once connected Africa and South America. The bridge was covered by water when the Atlantic Ocean formed.

This map shows South America and Africa during the time that Giganotosaurus and its relatives lived. The brown areas show mountains. The red dot shows where a Giganotosaurus fossil was discovered.

SOUTH AMERICA

AFRICA

GIGANOTOSAURUS BABIES

Even though Giganotosaurus grew to an enormous size, it was no more than a few inches long when it hatched. The young were helpless and were probably preyed upon by larger predators such as crocodiles.

A Giganotosaurus did not reach its full size until it was 20 years old. It usually died before age 30. That means its childhood was longer than its adulthood.

EASY FOOD

Even though Giganotosaurus was a fierce predator, it would eat the remains of large animals that had died of natural causes. A dead Rayosaurus, for example, could provide hundreds of pounds of meat. Eating a dead animal was much safer than attacking a live one.

Scientists believe an adult Giganotosaurus would have needed to eat around 44 pounds (20kg) of meat a day to survive. A young one would have needed only 10 pounds (4.6kg) or less.

Dangerous Prey

Because Giganotosaurus preyed on plant-eating animals much larger than itself, it had to be careful. It could be hurt badly by a blow of the tail or a kick from a prey animal. If it received an injury such as a broken leg that would not allow it to move, it would starve to death.

Once it made a kill, Giganotosaurus would have enough food to live on for weeks. So it did not have to hunt very often.

GIGANOTOSAURUS TRACKS

The borders of the lakes and rivers where Giganotosaurus lived were covered with mud and sand. When a Giganotosaurus wandered around looking for prey, it left the tracks of its large, three-toed hind feet in this mud. The mud dried in the sun and was later covered by more layers of mud and sand.

Over time, the upper layers pressed down on the lower ones, turning them into hard rocks. Those rocks are being unearthed today in Argentina. They show where these dinosaurs walked millions of years ago.

THE GIGANOTOSAURUS BODY

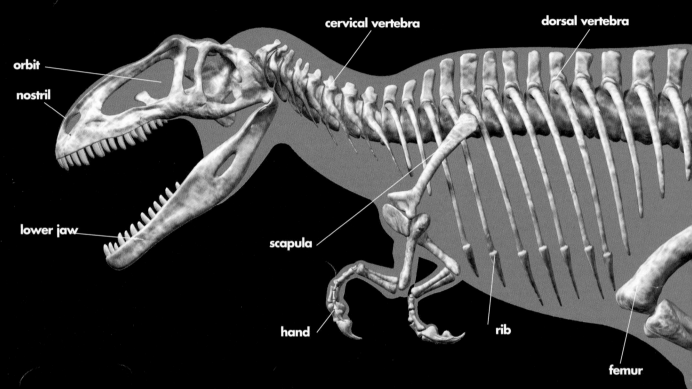

cervical vertebra

dorsal vertebra

orbit

nostril

lower jaw

scapula

hand

rib

femur

Scientists who have studied Giganotosaurus believe that the animal's skull was a little over 5 feet (1.6m) long. The teeth were up to 8 inches (20cm) long. They were curved with jagged edges. Giganotosaurus used these teeth to rip large pieces of meat from the body of its prey. It swallowed these pieces whole, without chewing.

The hind feet of a Giganotosaurus had three long toes with sharp claws and a smaller toe, or thumb, that did not touch the ground. Fossilized Giganotosaurus tracks show that this dinosaur did not drag its tail when it walked and that it moved fairly quickly.

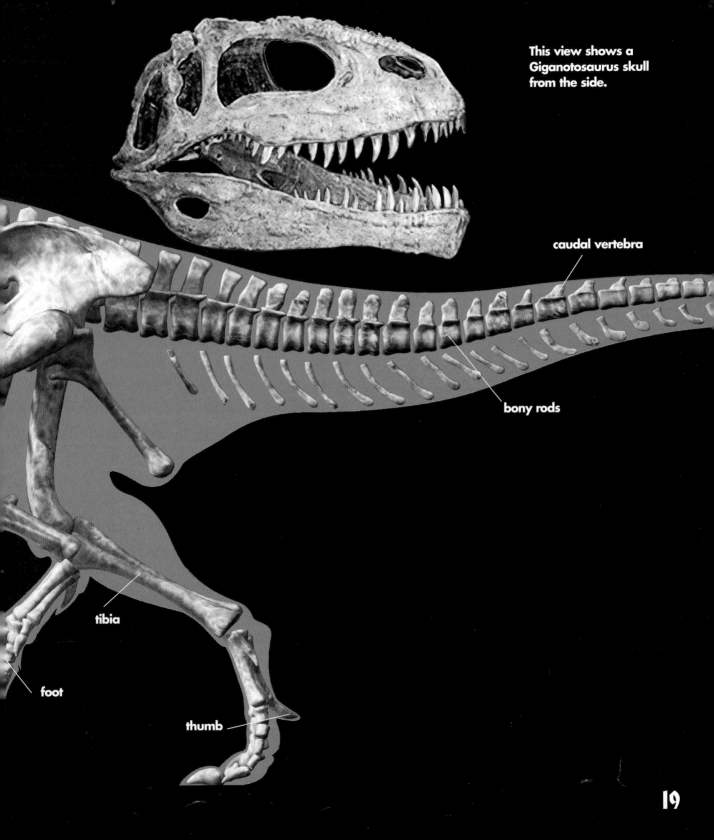

This view shows a
Giganotosaurus skull
from the side.

caudal vertebra

bony rods

tibia

foot

thumb

Digging Up Giganotosaurus

The first Giganotosaurus skeleton was discovered in July 1993 in an area of Argentina known today as the Valley of the Dinosaurs. The skeleton was found by Ruben Carolini, whose hobby was hunting fossils. Argentine paleontologists Rodolfo Coria and Leonardo Salgado gave the dinosaur its name in 1995. Today, the remains are on display in the town of Villa El Chocón, about 9 miles (15km) south of where the dinosaur was found. Models of the dinosaur are on display in other museums in Argentina and around the world.

The remains of Argentinosaurus, the largest known plant-eating dinosaur, were found only about 30 miles (50km) from where Giganotosaurus was discovered. However, Argentinosaurus lived hundreds of thousands or even a million years after Giganotosaurus, so the two never met.

Top: The huge Giganotosaurus skull has a rough surface and large, jagged teeth. The three clawed fingers were use to grasp prey.

Bottom: These Giganotosaurus tracks were made in ancient soft mud that over time turned to hard stone.

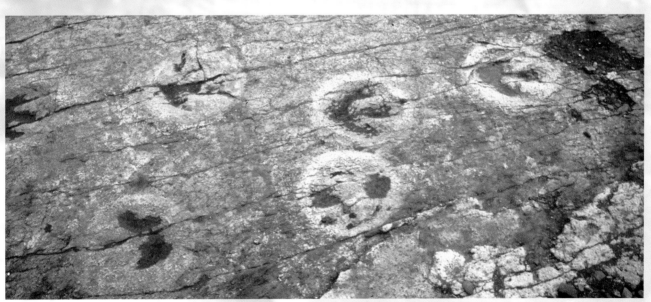

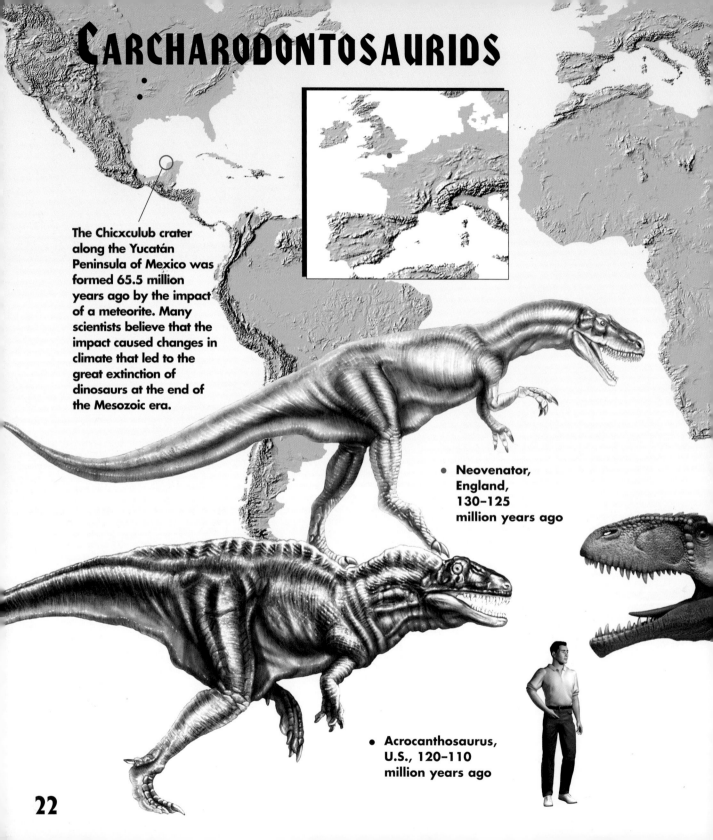

CARCHARODONTOSAURIDS

The Chicxculub crater along the Yucatán Peninsula of Mexico was formed 65.5 million years ago by the impact of a meteorite. Many scientists believe that the impact caused changes in climate that led to the great extinction of dinosaurs at the end of the Mesozoic era.

- Neovenator, England, 130–125 million years ago

- Acrocanthosaurus, U.S., 120–110 million years ago

The carcharodontosaurids, relatives of Giganotosaurus, were fairly common during the mid-Cretaceous period. Their name comes from the Greek and means "shark-toothed lizards."

Opposite: This map shows sites where the carcharodontosaurids pictured below have been found.

• **Carcharodontosaurus, North Africa, 100–90 million years ago**

• **Giganotosaurus, Argentina, 100–95 million years ago**

THE GREAT EXTINCTION

Sixty-five million years ago, around 25 million years after the time of Giganotosaurus, dinosaurs became extinct. This may have happened because a large meteorite struck Earth. A wide crater caused by a meteorite 65 million years ago has been located along the coast of the Yucatán Peninsula in Mexico. The impact of the meteorite would have produced an enormous amount of dust. This dust would have stayed suspended in the atmosphere and blocked sunlight for a long time. A lack of sunlight would have caused a drastic drop in Earth's temperature and killed plants. The plant-eating dinosaurs would have died, starved and frozen. As a result, meat-eating dinosaurs would have had no prey and would also have starved.

Some scientists believe dinosaurs did not die out completely. They think that birds were feathered dinosaurs that survived the great extinction. That would make the present-day chicken and all of its feathered relatives descendants of the large dinosaurs.

THE EVOLUTION OF DINOSAURS

The oldest dinosaur fossils are 220–225 million years old and have been found mainly in South America. They have also been found in Africa, India, and North America. Dinosaurs probably evolved from small and nimble bipedal reptiles like the Triassic Lagosuchus of Argentina. Dinosaurs were able to rule the world because their legs were held directly under the body, like those of modern mammals. This made them faster and less clumsy than other reptiles.

Since 1887, dinosaurs have been divided into two groups based on the structure of their hips. Saurischian dinosaurs had hips shaped like those of modern lizards. Ornithischian dinosaurs had hips shaped like those of modern birds.

Triceratops is one of the ornithischian dinosaurs, whose hip bones (inset) are shaped like those of modern birds.

Tyrannosaurus is in the saurischian group of dinosaurs, whose hip bones (inset) are shaped like those of modern lizards.

There are two main groups of saurischians. One group is sauropodomorphs. This group includes sauropods, such as Brachiosaurus. Sauropods ate plants and were quadrupedal, meaning they walked on four legs. The other group of saurischians, theropods, includes bipedal meat-eating predators. Some paleontologists believe birds are a branch of theropod dinosaurs.

Ornithischians are all plant eaters. They are divided into three groups. Thyreophorans include the quadrupedal stegosaurians, including Stegosaurus, and ankylosaurians, including Ankylosaurus. The other two groups are ornithopods, which includes Edmontosaurus and marginocephalians.

A DINOSAUR'S FAMILY TREE

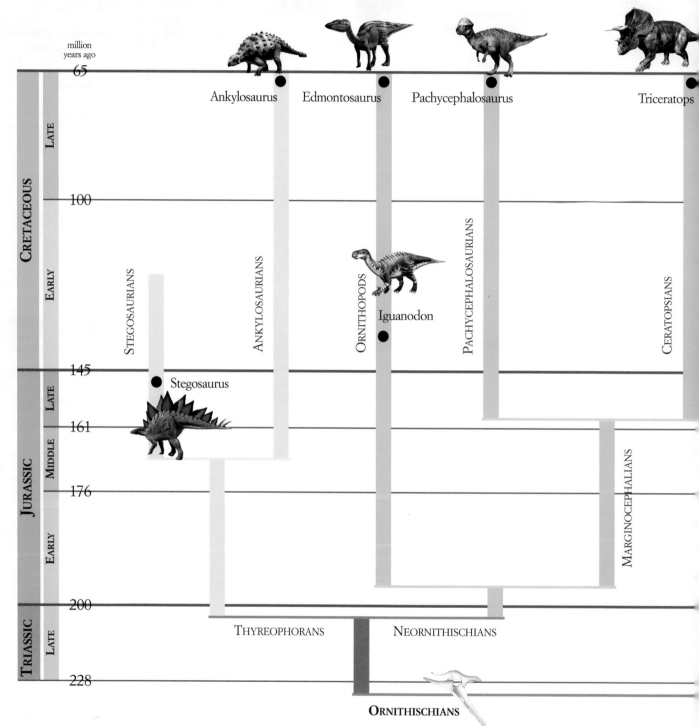

million years ago

65

100

145

161

176

200

228

CRETACEOUS

LATE

EARLY

JURASSIC

LATE

MIDDLE

EARLY

TRIASSIC

LATE

Ankylosaurus

Edmontosaurus

Pachycephalosaurus

Triceratops

STEGOSAURIANS

ANKYLOSAURIANS

ORNITHOPODS

PACHYCEPHALOSAURIANS

CERATOPSIANS

Iguanodon

Stegosaurus

MARGINOCEPHALIANS

THYREOPHORANS

NEORNITHISCHIANS

ORNITHISCHIANS

Ornithomimus

Tyrannosaurus

Velociraptor

ORNITHOMIMOIDEANS

TYRANNOSAUROIDS

OVIRAPTOROSAURIANS

DEINONYCHOSAURIANS

BIRDS

Giganotosaurus

Scipionyx

Deinonychus

SAUROPODS

Caudipteryx

Brachiosaurus ●● Diplodocus

Ornitholestes

THEROPODS

PROSAUROPODS

● Plateosaurus

ROPODOMORPHS

NOSAURIA   **SAURISCHIANS**

27

Glossary

Bipedal moving on two feet

Caudal related to the tail

Cervical related to the neck

Claws sharp, pointed nails on the fingers and toes of predators

Cretaceous period the period of geological time between 144 and 65 million years ago

Dorsal related to the back

Evolution changes in living things over time

Femur thigh bone

Fossil part of a living thing, such as a skeleton or leaf imprint, that has been preserved in Earth's crust from an earlier geological age

Jurassic period the period of geological time between 206 and 144 million years ago

Mesozoic era the period of geological time between 228 and 65 million years ago

Meteorite a piece of iron or rock that falls to Earth from space

Orbit the opening in the skull surrounding the eye

Paleontologist a scientist who studies prehistoric life

Predator an animal that hunts other animals for food

Prey an animal that is hunted by other animals for food

Quadrupedal moving on four feet

Skeleton the structure of an animal body, made up of bones

Skull the bones that form the head and face

Tibia shinbone

Triassic period the period of geological time between 248 and 206 million years ago

Vertebra a bone of the spine

FOR MORE INFORMATION

Books

Dougal Dixon, *Giganotosaurus and Other Big Dinosaurs.* Bloomington, MN: Picture Window Books, 2006.

Joanne Mattern, *Giganotosaurus.* Milwaukee, WI: Weekly Reader Early Learning Library, 2007.

Shelley Tanaka, *New Dinos.* New York: Atheneum, 2003.

Web Sites

Dinosaur Hall
http://www.ansp.org/museum/dinohall/index.php
This section of the Web site of the Academy of Natural Sciences in Philadelphia contains a picture of a Giganotosaurus skull along with information about it and other dinosaurs.

Giants of the Mesozoic
http://www.fernbank.edu/museum/giants.html
This section of the Web site of the Fernbank Museum of Natural History in Atlanta provides information about Giganotosaurus and Argentinosaurus.

The Smithsonian National Museum of Natural History
http://www.nmnh.si.edu/paleo/dino/
A virtual tour of the Smithsonian's National Museum of Natural History dinosaur exhibits.

About the Author

Fabio Marco Dalla Vecchia is the curator of the Paleontological Museum of Monfalcone in Gorizia, Italy. He has participated in several paleontological field works in Italy and other countries and has directed paleontological excavations in Italy. He is the author of more than 50 scientific articles that have been published in national and international journals.

INDEX

INDEX